YELLOWSTONE
AND
GRAND TETON
NATIONAL PARKS

Text by
TODD WILKINSON

Photographs by
ANDREA PISTOLESI

BONECHI
SNC

Distributed by

NORTHWEST NEWS - BILLINGS

711 4th Avenue North
Billings, Montana 59101
U.S.A.
Phone: 406 - 245-5784 - Fax: 406 - 245-0673

WELCOME TO YELLOWSTONE AND GRAND TETON NATIONAL PARKS

*Yellowstone and Grand Teton national parks
are two of the most beloved nature
preserves in the world. Located in the states
of northwest Wyoming, southern Montana,
and eastern Idaho, they are true
crown jewels in the
American National Park System.
As priceless vestiges of the primeval frontier,
each park is a powerful symbol
of the bond humans everywhere share with
the land. Together, renowned Italian
landscape photographer
Andrea Pistolesi and Bozeman, Montana
writer Todd Wilkinson take readers
on a fantastic journey to discover
the hidden treasures of Yellowstone and its
breathtaking neighbor, Grand Teton.
Whether you are exploring both parks
for the first time or making a return trip,
this photographic journal
provides a dramatic visual narrative
of your visit.*

INTRODUCTION

For thousands of years going back to the end of the Pleistocene Ice Age and the retreat of the mighty Wisconsin Glacial Period, Yellowstone National Park and its sister preserve, Grand Teton, have been places of profound mystery and intrigue to human explorers. The first people to recognize the incomparable beauty were American Indians passing through the parks on their way to hunt buffalo. We can only imagine the thoughts that nomadic tribesmen had upon seeing wonderful plumes of hot water being blown skyward by the eruptions of Yellowstone's 300 geysers. Or try to envision their speechless delight upon creeping to the edge of the Grand Canyon of the Yellowstone and witnessing a thundering waterfall—one of the largest on the continent—cascading into a rainbow mist.

One thing is absolutely certain: the Yellowstone region had a reputation among indigenous cultures that was far and wide. The reason is because the park yielded a coveted bounty of raw materials even more valuable than gold. At Obsidian Cliff in the heart of Yellowstone, ancient craftsmen quarried black obsidian rock from the rugged hillsides and fashioned it into sharp arrowheads and spear points crucial to the survival of palaeolithic Man. During archeological excavations in the 20th century, such weapons mined in Yellowstone were found dispersed thousands of miles away in sites as distant as the upper Ohio River valleys and the coastal hinterlands of the Pacific Ocean. Modern anthropologists believe that Yellowstone obsidian was a valuable commodity used in commerce and trading between indigenous peoples throughout North America. Strange as it may seem, it was obsidian, not pretty views, that first put Yellowstone on the map.

Still, as Indian traders returned time and again, it did not take long before the preternatural riches of Yellowstone became legendary. More than a dozen different tribes are affiliated geographically with the park but only one band of Indians—the "Sheepeaters"—actually resided there year round. These descendants of the Bannock-Shoshone Indian tribes were given their name because their diet consisted of meat taken from the park's resident bighorn sheep that still roam the high mountain slopes. While Yellowstone always has been known for its wildlife, some Native American tribes also revered the landscape as a place which emanated spiritual power. Visitors today regardless of their own religious backgrounds attest to experiencing the same feelings.

It was not until European settlers landed in North America after the arrival of Christopher Columbus that the rest of the world would learn of Yellowstone's uniqueness.

By the beginning of the 19th century, fur trappers and mountain men of French and British descent began telling stories about the Yellowstone region that seemed too outrageous to be true. They spoke of boiling rivers, fountains of gushing

In 1903, hundreds of people watched as a cornerstone was laid to commemorate the construction of a grand rock archway at Yellowstone's northern entrance.

An avid hunter and an early supporter of conservation efforts in the United States, Roosevelt made a special trip to Yellowstone and attended the ceremony where the arch was dedicated in his honor.

water and mud volcanoes which belched steam from hell. For a span of 40 years or so, interest in Yellowstone was overshadowed by the great migration of settlers to the states of California, Oregon and Washington. Yet, when the end of the American Civil War came in 1865, the country was again ready to turn its attention toward the wilderness interior. As interest grew to chart the strange anomalies of Yellowstone, the U.S. government began sending scientific expeditions to verify the old mountain men tales. Soon thereafter, Congress realized that Yellowstone was one-of-a-kind in its glory and needed protection forevermore.

When viewed as central contiguous pieces in a larger puzzle, Yellowstone and Grand Teton national parks represent the spiritual heart of the ''Greater Yellowstone ecosystem.''

Encompassing an area more than twice the size of Switzerland, this region in the northern Rocky Mountains is regarded as one of the largest expanses of unbroken wilderness left in the world's temperate zones. Ninety percent of the land mass in Greater Yellowstone is owned by the federal government of the United States. In 1972, exactly 100 years after Yellowstone was created, the United Nations declared the park environs as a World Biosphere Reserve, and six years later the U.N. added another distinction, that of World Heritage Site in honor of its ecological novelty. Yellowstone and Grand Teton are surrounded by seven national forests and three national wildlife refuges. In addition, the heavy snows which fall in the mountains become a major source of water for the Columbia, Colorado, and Missouri river systems. The watersheds themselves are poignant reminders of an interconnectedness beyond park boundaries. Like arteries circuiting through a human body, rivers are the lifeblood of the land and there are hundreds of streams flowing through Yellowstone and Grand Teton. In turn, the channels of water are a nexus for birds and mammals.

Over the years, poets and writers have celebrated the pristine character of both national parks but it was Theodore Roosevelt, a former U.S. President, hunter and explorer who declared without hesitation that the Yellowstone-Teton area was ''the most beautiful country in the world.''

Regardless of your taste in the outdoors, there is

Traveling through Yellowstone before the arrival of motorcars was always an adventure. Hotels in the park, like ''the National Hotel'' at Mammoth Hot Springs, were situated about a day's journey apart. Guests often came and stayed at the remote lodges for weeks at a stretch. Here, a group of tourists have piled onto a stagecoach which is leaving for one of the hotels in the interior of the park.

Before Mammoth Hot Springs became the official headquarters for park rangers, it was the site of Fort Yellowstone where the U.S. military took on caretaking responsibilities in the first decades of Yellowstone's existence. Army soldiers were summoned initially to combat poachers and bandits. In this 1913 photograph, Cavalry "F" Troop poses in front of its barracks.

Many of the roads that park visitors drive across today were originally built for stagecoach touring. All of the travel was done during the day and guides told harrowing stories about the fur trappers and mountain men who passed through Yellowstone early in the 19th century. Today, buses have replaced the stagecoaches but the sightseeing is equally as spectacular and a lot more comfortable.

Fishing Cone along the shore of Lake Yellowstone had an international reputation for many years. Tourists could stand on the neck of the cone, catch a trout in the lake and then lower the fish into the geyser cone to cook it.

something for everyone who comes here on vacation. Between them, Yellowstone and Grand Teton offer nearly 1,000 kilometers of hiking trails, superb rock climbing, exceptional canoe and kayak paddling and unmatched opportunities for observing wildlife.

Discovering the wonders of Yellowstone is a magical experience. It is possible to spend weeks in Yellowstone without feeling as though you have seen it all. And yet, tourists travelling in automobile or bus can see most of the main park features over the course of a day. Getting around Yellowstone is easy. The road system, called "The Grand Loop," is based upon a "figure 8" pattern that passes by such landmarks as Old

The most endearing residents of Yellowstone are, of course, its famous bears. In fact, the cartoon characters Yogi and Booboo which live in the fictional park of "Jellystone" are based upon bears observed in Yellowstone. Today, there are healthy populations of both grizzly bears and black bears in the park but it is rare to see massive bruins begging for food from humans. In the 1970s, park officials closed the food dumps and encouraged the bears to adopt an all-natural diet.

Faithful, Yellowstone Lake, the Grand Canyon of the Yellowstone and Mammoth Hot Springs. The most difficult decision awaiting the Yellowstone visitor is deciding where to begin the adventure. One essential sidetrip should include a drive through the Lamar Valley in the northeast corner of Yellowstone. The Lamar is a splendid, peaceful dell that was formed by melting glaciers thousands of years ago. Today, it is a prime retreat for professional wildlife watchers on safari with their cameras. The Lamar is part of a large mosaic of rolling hills and meadows known as the "Northern Range." Biologists liken the Northern Range to the Serengeti Plain in East Africa because both are resplendent with large wandering mammal populations. In Yellowstone, the list of animals that can be spied here includes elk, deer, moose, bison, pronghorn, grizzly bears, and coyotes. The newest animal to arrive in the valley are canine predators which were eliminated from Yellowstone in the late 1920s— grey wolves. As part of a novel reintroduction effort, 14 Canadian wolves were captured and released in the Lamar Valley early in 1995. The wild dogs appear to be enjoying their new home and have formed packs. Wildlife watching in Grand Teton can be equally as alluring, provided you find the time to take your eyes off the mountains which have a magnetic appeal. In Grand Teton, navigating the highway system is similarly hassle free. This park, too, can be toured in a single day but you won't be disappointed if you set aside several mornings and afternoons to trek through the Teton Mountains or camp beside one of the sparkling lakes. During the winter, a major portion of the highway system shuts down in both Yellowstone and Grand Teton but the parks remain accessible to visitors on snowmobiles and nordic skis.

GEOLOGY

The study of geology often implies a static, sedentary landscape that is part of ancient history. In Yellowstone and Grand Teton, the ground lying at your fee still is very active. Mountains are being made and new hot springs bubble up almost every year. The best part of all this is that even on a grand geologic scale covering billions of years, we are able to witness some of the changes taking place in our own lifetimes.

Yellowstone and Grand Teton are renowned for their geological expressions but for different reasons. Fire and ice have played vital roles in sculpting the topography. While the parks share some common influences, the beauty of each preserve has its own origins. With more than 10,000 geothermal features contained inside its borders—more than the rest of the world combined—Yellowstone is considered a major geologic "hotspot." Superheated magma located just a few miles beneath the Earth's surface has molded the landscape above ground. Yellowstone is special because its geysers, hot springs, mud volcanoes, fumaroles and boiling rivers still function naturally, which is to say humans have let them be. Elsewhere in the world, similar magnificent resources have been destroyed by human development.

To trace the genesis of the modern Yellowstone requires taking a trip through time. The first hints of Yellowstone's legacy as a major hotspot began to emerge 50 million years ago.The Absaroka mountains which tower above the eastern reaches of the park, were built by volcanoes spewing lava and ash. They are the first building blocks in the formation of the Yellowstone Plateau which ranges between 7,000 and 8,000 feet (2,134 and 2,438m) above sea level. The upwelling of fired rock produced the high, snowcapped peaks seen over the eastern shore of Yellowstone Lake. During this same time span, mudflows buried ancient tropical forests and left behind petrified trees seen in the northern sections of the park. The show of fire

Beaver ponds are places that attract some of the greatest diversity of animal life in Yellowstone. By the end of the 19th century, beaver had been virtually eliminated from many parts of the American West but today the furbearing animals are returning to reclaim their former niches.

The Continental Divide ultimately determines whether water from a raindrop or snowflake flows west toward the Pacific Ocean or east toward the Gulf of Mexico. In Yellowstone, the Continental Divide, dubbed the backbone of America, is deluged by heavy snowfall during the long winter months.

probably continued for a few million years more until a series of mega-scale volcanic eruptions lit up the sky and shook the ground, each one epic in its dimensions. After periodic spans of relative quiet, the earth awoke again with a fury.

The latest crescendo occurred about 600,000 years ago. In a violent rage that would dwarf any volcanic eruption of the 20th century, a giant volcano exploded, leaving behind a crater 28 miles wide and 47 miles long (45 X 76 km). The impression of that blast still is visible in the outline of the Yellowstone caldera. It left trenches of ash hundreds of miles downwind. While the landscape today may appear restful at last, a similar eruption theoretically could occur again but there are no indications that it will happen anytime soon.

Besides being a hotspot, Yellowstone is active seismically as well. Each year swarms of minor earthquakes shake the ground, though the vast majority go undetected by people on the surface. Earthquakes, however, do have a profound effect on the natural underground pipes that feed the geysers and hot springs. As old vents of steam and boiling water are rendered extinct, new pools and geysers rise up in their place.

Scientists have compared the active crust of Yellowstone to a candle slowly being pulled beneath a sheet of cloth. As the fire below moves across the landscape, it exposes the surface to a wide array of geothermal phenomena. There are three primary thermal areas in the park—The Upper and Midway geyser basins, the Norris Geyser Basin, and the travertine terraces at Mammoth Hot Springs.

Meanwhile, in Grand Teton Park, the lofty peaks of the Teton Range have retained their toothy appearance because they are made of hard · granite, which is resistant to the erosive forces of wind and water. What makes the Tetons especially interesting is this: While the granitic, metamorphic gneiss and schist that comprise the mountain range is among the oldest-known rock on earth (as old as three billion years), the Tetons at nine million years old are the youngest peaks in the Rocky Mountains which are believed to be about 60 million years old. The paradox can be explained through the geologic process called ''uplifting.'' Interestingly, the first manifestation of the Tetons produced

The collection of geysers, hot springs, bubbling mud volcanoes and steamy fumaroles makes Yellowstone a prime geologic hotspot. Indeed, the 10,000 geothermal phenomena found in the park represent more than are found in the rest of the world.

smooth mountain tops. At one time perhaps nine million years ago,the Tetons were actually part of a flat plain. But over the ages violent movement began to occur between two massive blocks of earth that intersected along the Teton Fault. The fault is about 40 miles (65 km) long.

Through earthquakes and other factors, the fault blocks on the eastern face of the Tetons began to dip while the western side of the mountains began to rise. The total vertical displacement has been 30,000 feet (9,000 m). This explains the lowness of the Jackson Hole valley compared to the highness of the peaks. This same type of phenomenon occurred throughout the entire Rocky Mountain front. Even today, the Tetons still are slowly growing. By one estimate, the eastern fault block in Jackson Hole has sunken four times deeper than the mountains above it have climbed. Each year, the summit of the Grand Teton and other peaks get a little taller and may grow at the rate of several inches (centimeters) every century. Like the potential awakening of the Yellowstone caldera, the fault line which flanks the foot of the Tetons east of Jenny Lake is capable of producing a massive earthquake of 7.5 on the magnitude scale. The final touch in the Tetons' appearance came between 20,000 and 60,000 years ago when glaciers carved out bowls, cirques, moraines, and canyons. The glaciers you see pressed into the east and northern aspects of the mountains today are related to those sheets of ice. Rather, they are comprised of snow which collected during cooler weather over the past couple of thousand years.

Another influence of geology that affects Yellowstone and Grand Teton is the Continental Divide. This crest of the Rocky Mountains has been called the backbone of western America but in practical terms its greatest impact is on water. When a snowflake or raindrop falls in the mountains, its ultimate path is determined by whether it is on the east or west side of the Continental Divide. All water on the east side of the divide embarks on a journey toward the Gulf of Mexico, a body of water in the Atlantic Ocean. Moisture gathered west of the Divide flows toward the Pacific Ocean. Generally, the climate west of the Divide is wetter and warmer while conditions east of the Divide tend to be dryer and cooler.

You don't have to be academically trained in geology to appreciate the profound natural wonders in Yellowstone and Grand Teton national parks. From Old Faithful to the Tetons, there is a lifetime's worth of fascinating topography to explore.

THE FIRES OF 1988

In 1988, conditions in Yellowstone were ripe for an epic inferno. And then Mother Nature provided the spark. Lack of rainfall, combined with hot temperatures, brisk winds, and frequent lightning strikes caused more than a dozen major forest fires to rage across one-third of the park. At least $120 million was spent battling the blazes and trying to save historic log buildings from being destroyed. The burning of Yellowstone made news around the world and many people feared that perhaps the park was dead. But like a Phoenix rising from the ashes, the park landscape, ecologically speaking, has undergone a profound rebirth. Portions of Yellowstone which used to have dark pine canopies now are bursting with wildflowers, grasses, and new trees. The profusion of vegetation, in turn, has provided a bounty of forage for animals ranging in size from tiny mouselike voles to elk and one-ton bison. Even fish have benefitted from nutrients which have been washed into the streams. Park visitors can see dramatic evidence of the 1988 fires around Old Faithful, Canyon Village, Mammoth Hot Springs, Norris Geyser Basin and Roosevelt Lodge.

The forest fires which swept across much of Yellowstone in 1988 were of historic magnitude but they also sparked an ecological rebirth in the park. It will be witnessed by human visitors for many generations to come.

WILDLIFE

Animal lovers from around the world visit the Greater Yellowstone region each year to embark upon nature safaris with their cameras. Indeed, the opportunity to see North American game animals is incomparable. Here you will find the largest free-roaming herds of bison and elk in the United States and habitat for over 60 species of mammals and 260 species of birds. Well over half of the birds are neotropical migrants that spend their winters in the warm climates of Latin America before returning to the forests and waterways of the northern Rocky Mountains to breed in the spring. During the 20th century, Yellowstone, Grand Teton and the adjacent wildlands played an important role in the survival of several animals, including the grizzly bear, grey wolf, trumpeter swan, bald eagle, peregrine falcon and pure genetic strains of fish. Because of its abundant wildlife, the Greater Yellowstone region has been called "a true vignette of primitive America."

The growing season (upper right) in Yellowstone is brief but for about five months beginning in late April, plants push out of the snowpack and bud new leaves. While the region around Yellowstone is dominated by pine trees, aspens turn fiery with blazing orange and yellow hues in September and October. The autumn is a quiet and relaxing season to enjoy both Yellowstone and Grand Teton.

One of Yellowstone's many grizzly bears and a beautiful specimen of a bald eagle.

11

A

B

C

D

E

(A) A bull elk bugling in autumn
(B) A growing yearling bison
(C) A coyote hunting for a rodent snack
(D) Bison grazing near an erupting geyser
(E) A pair of sparring bull moose
(F) Elk in snow
(G) Young elk playing in a pond
(H) Canada geese find protection on a rock island

The environment of Yellowstone and Grand Teton national parks contains some of the highest concentrations of large wild animals in the world.

G

F

H

YELLOWSTONE

NATIONAL PARK

Y-e-l-l-o-w-s-t-o-n-e. The origin of the word is owed to French fur trappers who took notice of the yellowish rocks that flanked the Yellowstone River. Within international science circles, however, the name is considered an icon of conservation. Indeed, when most people think of Yellowstone they picture "the mother of all national parks" because it was here that the idea of national parks was born. On March 2, 1872, the Congress of the United States set aside Yellowstone as the first national park in the world. Since that time, the concept of national parks has spread worldwide. Today, parks based upon the Yellowstone model now exist in more than 100 nations across the globe.

For visitors who pass beneath the park's stone archway at Gardiner, Montana, the motto of Yellowstone says it all: For the Enjoyment and Benefit of the People.The efficient and comfortable methods of touring the park today are vastly different from the those that greeted the first tourists. During the latter part of the 19th century, Yellowstone was still very much a destination in the wild West. In the early days, long before the invention of the automobile, visitors toured the park in stage coaches and some of them occasionally confronted armed bandits. Eventually, law and order prevailed when military soldiers were stationed at Fort Yellowstone (today Mammoth Hot Springs) to guard against thieves and poachers. Today, there are many who believe that saving this 2.2-million-acre (829,600 hectare) preserve as a gift to citizens everywhere was the best idea Americans ever had. Foremost, Yellowstone was created to protect its geysers and wildlife. To grasp the importance of Yellowstone is to understand its place in history. At the time of its creation, Yellowstone was a bold, radical declaration, to be sure. As the limits of the American frontier were being realized, it became clear that without protection, special places would not endure for future generations.

The brilliance of Yellowstone is found in the fact that more than a century later, the resources inside its boundary still summon a sense of wonder to three million visitors who experience them each year.

In recent years, the wisdom of those who supported the protection of Yellowstone has become more and more evident. From the hot springs has emerged major scientific discoveries such as the technology that resulted in DNA fingerprinting. As a wildlife reservoir, the park has been a vital sanctuary for imperiled species. The bison herds you pass in the Hayden and Lamar valleys are descendants of fewer than 100 wild animals rescued from poachers at the end of the 19th century. Scarcely a few hundred years ago, biologists estimate that as many 60 million bison thundered across the Great Plains but market hunters nearly pushed the species to extinction. Yellowstone became pivotal in saving them from such an unthinkable fate. Yellowstone has been integral to the recovery of elk numbers across the West. And trumpeter swans. And wolves. And, of course, its best-known wildlife inhabitants, bears.

Generations of children worldwide have viewed cartoons featuring the travails of Yogi and Booboo in a fictional park called Jellystone. Creators of the cartoon based their characters on bears in Yellowstone. Two species inhabit the park: black bears, and the much bigger grizzly bears (a cousin of the European brown bear). Black bears are fairly common in the U.S. but grizzlies are rare and afforded special protection under federal law. Yellowstone is one of only two places in the lower 48 states where grizzlies still survive in self-sustaining populations. At present, more than 300 grizzlies are thought to exist in the Yellowstone region, though their survival is threatened by poachers, development such as logging, drilling for oil, and encroaching civilization that effects their habitat. Will grizzlies endure? That question remains to be answered.

UPPER GEYSER BASIN

Encountering Yellowstone's Upper Geyser Basin for the first time is a surreal and enchanting experience. This is the premier outpost in the world for observing active geysers. Nowhere else compares to the remarkable collection of subterranean vents which pipe up hot water from the fiery belly of the earth. Set against the backdrop of the meandering Firehole River, this basin is home to more than two dozen geysers whose vaporous clouds appear to dance like misty gossamers across the pristine landscape. Moving in and out of the fog are elk, buffalo, and sometimes even grizzly bears. Included within this remarkable collection of geysers are Old Faithful, Giant and Giantess, Daisy, Riverside, and the reflection of Morning Glory Pool. Nine out of

ten visitors travel to this busy corner of the park and many of them begin their journey at the Old Faithful Visitor Center where park rangers offer information about the next eruptions of local geysers. There is enough to see and do here to keep a traveler busy for many days. From Geyser Hill, visitors can set out to explore the Castle Grand Group, the Daisy Group, the Giant-Grotto Group and the Morning Glory-Riverside Group, each one with an unusual and distinctive array of geothermal activity. While walking through fields of immaculate fountains and translucent pools remember that you are witnessing the very same splendors that enthralled Native Americans long before the United States was even a nation.

As this map of the Upper Geyser Basin shows, the Old Faithful Area has plenty of attractions to see and explore. One of the best ways to plan a tour of the numerous geyser fields is to stop in at the Old Faithful Visitor Center and talk with park rangers who are geyser experts.

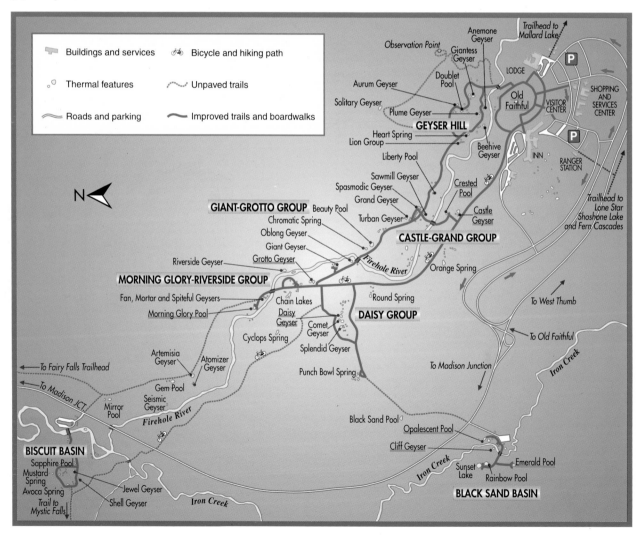

The Old Faithful Inn has the majesty of an old ship and inside (right) its vaulted ceiling is like a cathedral in the Wild West. This historic hotel overlooks several famous geysers, including Old Faithful, and is open from spring until the middle of autumn.

OLD FAITHFUL

OLD FAITHFUL INN

Rising like a wooden fortress above Old Faithful Geyser is a 327-room hotel that historians consider a architectural masterpiece. The Old Faithful Inn was designed in the tradition of the grand old hotels found throughout the American West. Many consider it to be the highlight of any stay in the park. Overlooking Old Faithful Geyser and the Upper Geyser Basin, the Inn provides immediate access to a boardwalk footpath that winds through Geyser Hill. On warm summer days, you can even sit on the hotel's outdoor patio and watch the geyser go off.

After a day spent touring the park, the lobby of the Inn makes for a peaceful retreat before dinner. The Inn has a spacious yet cozy feel to it. American Presidents have spent the night here and so, too, have visiting diplomats and celebrities. Inside the main entrance, a fireplace vaults toward the ceiling and surrounding it are pine logs, each one carefully selected to create an ornateness not found in other hotels. The Inn was built during the winter of 1903-04 under the vision of architect Robert Reamer and is listed on the National Register of Historic Places. Many of the beams came from trees cut down inside the park, including the planks stretching across the massive floor. At night, guests assemble on the second and third floors to read favorite books and write postcards to their friends back home.

While the design is considered priceless, the hotel was nearly destroyed. In 1988, a raging forest fire swept down from the surrounding mountain slopes and literally jumped over the roof. Remnants from that historic blaze still can be seen in the landscape today. The hotel is closed during the winter but open from May until the end of September. Accommodations during the winter are available at the nearby Snow Lodge. To rent a room you should make reservations well in advance of your stay.

OLD FAITHFUL GEYSER

No visit to Yellowstone is complete without a stop at its most famous icon, Old Faithful Geyser. Old Faithful isn't the biggest geyser in the park, nor is it necessarily the most spectacular, but it does attract big crowds. The reason may be because its legendary eruptions are generally predictable (but non exact) and dramatic. Like clockwork, (between 20 and 23 times every day), Old Faithful sends a plumb of hot water skyward much to the delight of adoring tourists who gather on the boardwalks encircling its cone.

The intervals between eruptions have ranged anywhere between 33 minutes and 120 minutes, though the vast majority occur every 70 minutes or so. This is especially impressive since some scientists believe Old Faithful has been active for 25,000 years! Prior to the start of an eruption, water fills a natural underground chamber. As the water is heated past the boiling point, pressure builds forcing the water and steam to spout above ground. Depending upon how much water fills the chamber, the height of the eruptions can vary. The tallest recorded eruption has been 184 feet and the shortest 106 feet. Just p rior to the eruption, the earth shakes and a roar can be heard deep in the ground. Over the years, Old Faithful has been threatened by vandalism from tourists who attempt to toss objects into its vent. Even throwing something as seemingly inane as a coin can cause problems with the natural underground plumbing system that feeds the geysers. The objects become lodged in the delicate vents and can plug them.

Old Faithful is the most famous geyser in the world and erupts, on average, about every 90 minutes. It is a focal point within the Upper Geyser Basin.

GEYSER HILL

With bison (better known as buffalo) wandering between columns of rising steam, and the pungent smell of sulfur thick in the air, a trek across Geyser Hill bestows tourists with a sense of awe. Geyser Hill encompasses a cluster of geysers and hot springs. Located directly across the Firehole River from the Old Faithful development, the hill itself is made accessible via a nature trail that runs across a boardwalk into open meadows that often are alive with buffalo and howling coyotes. Strolling along the trial, visitors often see at least one geyser erupt and possibly more—some even going off at the same time. The Geyser Hill Nature Trail is short and skirts such landmarks as Giantess Geyser, Doublet Pool, Plume Geyser and Heart Spring. Giantess is the largest of geysers in the Geyser Hill area. When it erupts the plume is large. All geysers in the park have been affected by past earthquakes. Although it seems unbelievable, even earthquakes in California more than 1,000 miles away can influence the eruption patterns of Yellowstone's geysers.

 Giantess is known to emit four different kinds of eruptions involving water and steam. Hikers who want a more challenging trek can stroll to the top of Observation Point and achieve a commanding view of not only Geyser Hill but forest behind it which was burned by a forest fire in 1988. Sunsets from Observation Point are fantastic. Remember that it is wise to stay on established trails because the Upper Geyser Basin is fragile.

Geyser Hill refers to a misty expanse of the Upper Geyser Basin where buffalo and coyotes intermingle with an array of hot springs, geysers, and fumaroles. Here, a boardwalk guides visitors into a wonderland of geothermal activity.

After touring Geyser Hill (above), many visitors embark on a stroll past other distinct geyser groups, including the one which is home to Castle Geyser (right), so named by explorers because they thought its cone resembled a Medieval fortress. It also shows that the first tourists in the park had creative imaginations.

CASTLE GEYSER

On a chilly morning, it is possible to literally disappear into the inveigling steam that shrouds Castle Geyser.Castle Geyser has the largest sinter cone of any geyser in the park and its recorded fountain of water ranks among the largest in the Castle Geyser Group not far from Old Faithful. The explorers who named all of the geothermal phenomena in Yellowstone obviously had vivid imaginations. In 1870, two members of the famed Washburn Expedition sent to catalog Yellowstone's geysers, suggested that the huge cone of Castle Geyser resembled "an old feudal tower partially in ruins." Although the comment exaggerates the size of the cone, the description underestimates its colorful charm and intriguing abstract shape. Unfortunately, the size of Castle's cone was once much bigger but tourists over the years have chipped away at its geyserite surface. The apron of water that spills away from the geyser is glassed by its own

patinas. All of the geysers in Yellowstone are, in effect, mini ecosystems brimming with a multitude of microscopic life forms. Growing in the pools beneath Castle is a spectrum of different bacteria and algae species that each cast off a different hue. Castle boasts eruptions that can reach 100 feet and the hot water brings minerals to the microorganisms growing in the pools. Nearby, Grand Geyser is another major geyser in the same group. Separated from Castle Geyser by the Firehole River, Grand also is the king of its own geyser group and has been known in the recent past as "the tallest predictable geyser on the planet." When Grand erupts, it always seizes the attention of visitors in the Old Faithful area. Over the course of its documented life, Grand has shown signs that it may be slowing down. While all geysers may look the same there are definite peculiarities in their behavior.

Every geothermal feature in Yellowstone has its own personality and the trio of Crested Pool, Grotto Geyser and Daisy Geyser are no exception. Crested Pool holds a trademark lip encircling its spring, Grotto Geyser comes alive in a moody splash of hot water, and the eruptions at Daisy Geyser always attract a crowd.

CRESTED POOL

The placid surface of Crested Pool invites the onlooker to peer deeper into an emerald green-blue abyss. Rimmed by silica, the walls of this intriguing pond shine as if they were made of sculpted white marble sinking 42 feet into the ground. Don't be fooled by Crested Pool's tranquil appearance. The water in this cauldron is hot! In 1970, a young boy died from burns when he unwisely decided to take a swim. Although the geothermal features in Yellowstone may look inviting, don't be fooled. Since 1872 when Yellowstone was created many several park visitors and their pets have suffered mortal injuries by jumping into scalding water. At the high elevations of the park, water can actually boil at temperatures which are a few degrees cooler.

GROTTO GEYSER

Not far away from Crested Pool is the moody, splashing effervescence of Grotto Geyser, which is the namesake for a whole group of gushers.

Grotto was celebrated by the famous Washburn Expedition in 1870 which submitted a report to Congress that ultimately convinced lawmakers to set aside Yellowstone as a national park. Grotto Geyser is remarkable because its eruptions can last for as long as 12 hours and reach heights of 40 feet.

DAISY GEYSER

Similar to Grotto Geyser, Daisy Geyser is the focal point for a distinct grouping of geysers and hot springs within the Upper Geyser Basin. Upon reaching Daisy, hikers can continue walking up the footpath to Punch Bowl Spring. In wintertime, nordic skiers glide across the frozen snowpack to reach Punch Bowl and then walk on bare ground. Each summer a group of specially-trained citizens come to Yellowstone to help park rangers record the eruptions of geysers. The people are known as "Geyser Gazers" and have chronicled significant changes in the rate of eruptions and size of regular water bursts.

A cauldron of translucent color, Morning Glory Pool possesses a magical allure and it has been a favorite attraction of Yellowstone visitors dating back to the 19th century.

MORNING GLORY POOL

Fresh as a blossoming wildflower, the aquamarine wash of Morning Glory Pool is imminently photogenic. As one of the most alluring geothermal springs in Yellowstone, Morning Glory basks in a prism of color. The circular bowl is filled with clear blue water and holds the appearance of a chalice.

This glowing pool was named after the morning glory flower which becomes ever more radiant with the rising sun. Indeed, nature photographers often arrive before dawn to set up their tripods and catch the first glistening rays of sunlight dancing across the pool. As the sunbeams pour into the small terrestrial impression, Morning Glory radiates warmth and seems energized.

Despite its popularity, Morning Glory has suffered from much vandalism over the years. The golden sinter brim which gave the pool an ornate appearance was chipped away by tourists who tried to take a piece of it home with them. Harming any feature in Yellowstone is illegal. The problem of plugging geysers and hot springs is that it causes them to cool or even go extinct. In the past few years, park rangers have floated a special boat across the surface of several hot springs to fish out debris. Among the objects pulled from the subterranean drainpipes were coins, shoes, bullets, eyeglasses, watches and even bones from animals that haphazardly waded in.

BLACK SAND BASIN

OPALESCENT POOL

From a distance, the setting of Black Sand Basin is eerie and otherworldly. Once upon a time a forest grew here but all that stands today are the barren trunks of trees which were engulfed by the encroaching tide of Opalescent Pool. Trees cannot survive in the sulfurous water and their roots literally are cooked by the high temperatures. At sunset when the whole of Black Sand Basin basks in the reddish rays of alpenglow, this complex of hot springs is shrouded in billowing exhalations of Spouter Geyser. The soil here has turned is so mineralized that most green plants cannot grow yet during the winter time the snow melts on contact with the ground. A variety of animals seek refuge from the cold temperatures but without forage to sustain them, many animals die. In the spring, the carcasses of elk and bison provide a windfall for hungry grizzly bears emerging from their dens after a long winter dormancy. The name Black Sand Basin was chosen because there are millions of tiny obsidian pebbles present in the sand. Opalescent Pool is located on the south side of the main highway near Cliff Geyser and Black Sand Pool is situated north of the highway. Black Sand Basin is one of the first clusters of geysers and hot springs that visitors encounter as they enter the Upper Geyser Basin.

Girded by totems of old pine trees, Opalescent Pool in the Black Sand Basin has a mysterious charm, especially at sundown when the fading light casts the steam into pink and red veils.

With dusk approaching (at left) columns of steam evoke a sense of primal awe. Meantime, Cliff Geyser (above) flanks the meandering course of a river in the Upper Geyser Basin.

EMERALD POOL and CLIFF GEYSER

Emerald Pool and Cliff Geyser are two easily-recognized features in the Black Sand Geyser Basin. Both of these remarkable features are accessible and located near the road. A liquid gem, Emerald Pool is popular among professional and amateur photographers because the hues radiating from it are clear and vivid. Many different kinds of algae and bacteria survive in the scalding water. Recent discoveries suggest that the type of microbes and tiny organisms inhabiting Yellowstone's hot springs are among the oldest in the world and may offer clues about how life began billions of years ago. Emerald Pool shares the crowds with nearby Rainbow Pool and off the beaten path a little further (actually tucked away from tourists) is Handkerchief Pool. For many years, tourists were allowed to drop handkerchiefs, coins and other trinkets into the iridescent natural wonder and watch them disappear briefly into the ground before being churned up again. Eventually, tossing such sacrificing items into Handkerchief destroyed it and only through some extensive removal of debris did it come back to life. Many things have changed in Yellowstone since the early days and one of them is a growing respect for how delicate and priceless the park's geothermal treasures are. Throwing foreign objects into any pool is strictly prohibited. Down the road from Emerald and Rainbow pools is the frothing surface of Cliff Geyser. A tiny wall of rock is the only obstacle separating it from Iron Spring Creek. The stream runs with a reddish tint but the color is not attributed to iron in the water as 19th century explorers first thought. Rather, it is reddish-brown algae that gives it a strange appearance. When Cliff Geyser turns active, it throws a spray of water into the river.

Green Pool is a liquid emerald gem whose water hovers constantly near the boiling point and strikes a stunning contrast against the turquoise-colored sky. The hues in the pool are owed to different species of bacteria and algae that can survive at hot temperatures.

MIDWAY GEYSER BASIN

Cast into the last remains of daylight, the Midway Geyser Basin marks a dramatic intersection of earth and sky. Found halfway between the Upper and Lower Geyser Basins on the west side of Yellowstone, Midway has assumed several names over the years. The famous writer Rudyard Kipling, who visited the park in 1889, referred to this frenetic geyser field as "Hell's Half Acre." While Kipling's prosaic description implies a landscape resembling Hades, Midway in fact overwhelms visitors' senses with a heavenly veil of ethereal fog and glowing sunsets. Several geothermal features can be witnessed at the same time. By walking a brief distance to Bluff Point from the Midway parking area, you can gain a commanding view of the main attractions in the basin—Grand Prismatic Spring, Turquoise Pool and Excelsior Geyser. A veritable dynamo, Excelsior was one of Yellowstone's most exciting geysers, unleashing a shower of water 300 feet high and an equal distance wide. For now, however, Excelsior Geyser lies in a state of dormancy, having erupted only a handful of times over the last century. The last time it pushed water into the sky, in 1983, the force was so great that it blew itself apart. Nonetheless, a lot of hot water still flows from its cone—as much as 1 1/2 billion gallons each year. According to geologists, the water which surfaces may have fallen as raindrops or snowflakes hundreds of years ago. That's how long it takes moisture to percolate into the ground and find its way into the geothermal plumbing system. The steam you see in the geyser basin is caused by scalding water making contact with cool air. Although Yellowstone is buried during the winter under many meters of snow, you can still find green grass growing in the Midway Geyser Basin during the deep freeze of January. As a result, elk and bison converge here to get easy meals. They, in turn, attract coyotes, wolves and grizzly bears in the spring. The predators wait for the old and feeble animals to die, then consume them. In Yellowstone, nothing goes to waste. Death is an important part of life.

While there are no written records of their visit, we can only speculate (page 28) what the first visitors to Yellowstone—the Native American Indians—thought about the strange wonders of Yellowstone. Upon trekking to the edge of some boiling pools (above), one gets the sensation of exploring the clouds. For fishermen (below) the Firehole River is legendary not only for its trout but the scenery is something that always outweighs the catch.

Once the water is expunged from the geysers and hot springs, it either seeps back into the ground or drains into the nearby Firehole River. Water reaching the surface of the ground in all of the geyser basins carries with it a rich mixture of nutrients. The minerals feed not only aquatic plants but provide sustenance for legendary populations of cutthroat trout. Don't be surprised as you drive through the Midway Geyser Basin if you see legions of anglers casting a line into this meandering stream. Fishermen from around the world come here to try and catch them. The maxim for anglers is the poorer the weather the more active the trout. The Firehole flows in a northern direction from Madison Lake near the Continental Divide toward its confluence with the Madison River. It takes its name from several explorers who proclaimed that the valley holding the geysers was filled with smoke. A more colloquial name for the Firehole is "river of geysers." Certain stretches of the Firehole run very warm and do not ice over even during the coldest of months.

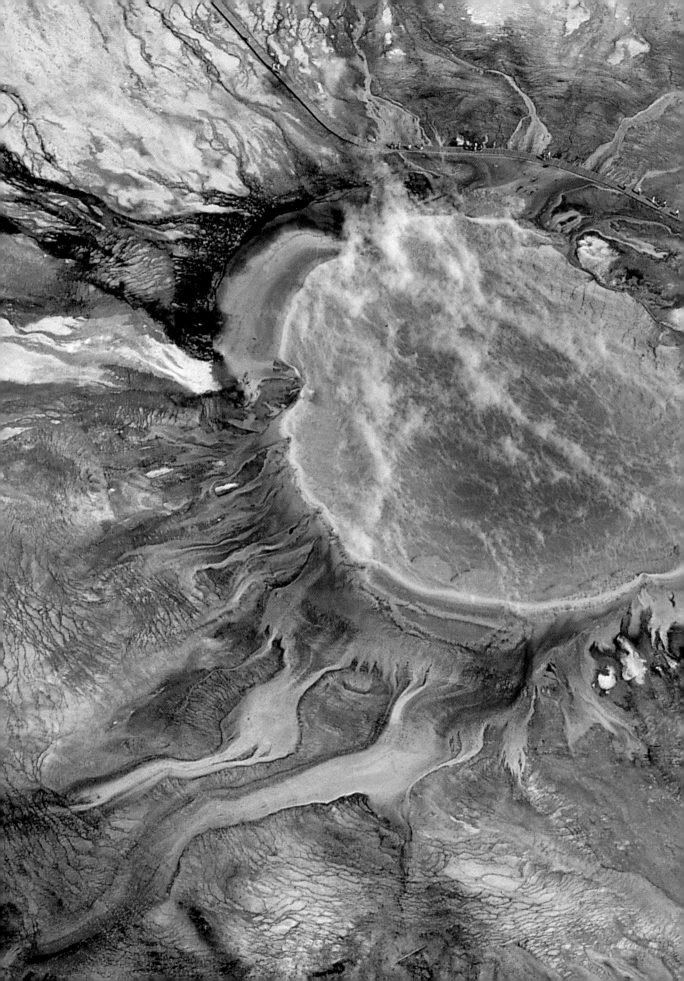

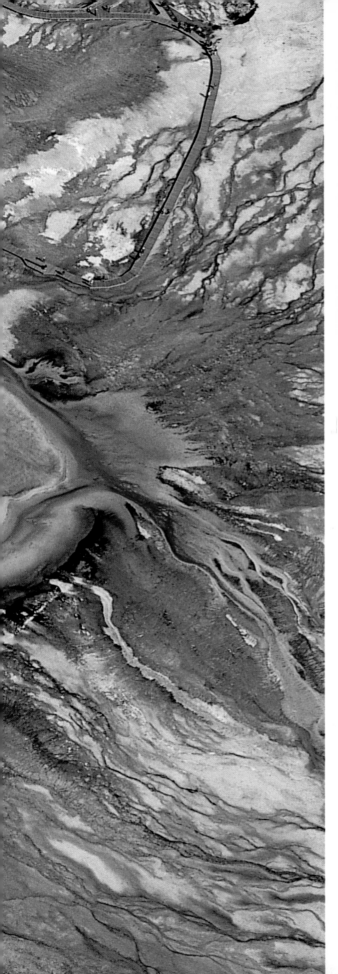

The sunburst pattern of Grand Prismatic Spring illustrates the enormity and natural splendor of this pool which holds a prism of color.

GRAND PRISMATIC SPRING

From the sky, the outline of Grand Prismatic Spring resembles a giant sunburst pattern flaring out from Yellowstone's Midway Geyser Basin. Bursting with color, the circular pool has azure blue at its central core surrounded by pastel green, yellow and fiery orange. Here, nature has created a very unique artist's pallet. The colors are influenced by different species of algae that thrive in different water temperatures. Grand Prismatic Spring, covering 370 feet in diameter, is the largest hot spring in Yellowstone and certainly the most spectacular. Scientists say it is part of the Excelsior Geyser Group. In 1871, American artist Thomas Moran completed a painting of the spring and displayed it before the Congress of the United States. Visitors can gain an intimate glimpse of the spring from a nearby footpath. Because the ground is always warm, it never freezes over with snow. At midday (above), the sun reflects off a crust of travertine that glistens in a wash of mineral water. The crust is very thin and brittle making it necessary that tourists remain on established boardwalks.

LOWER GEYSER BASIN

CLEPSYDRA GEYSER

It can be confusing trying to explain the logic which went into identifying the Lower Geyser Basin and the Upper Geyser Basin on a map. The "lower" basin is actually located to the north, and the "upper" basin to the south around Old Faithful. Lower, however, does not make this collection of geysers any less fantastic. Take, for example, the visage of Clepsydra Geyser. By now you have probably noticed that all of the geysers in Yellowstone bear names and each one has its own special history. Clepsydra is not exception to the rule. Encompassed by the Fountain Group of geysers, this constantly active body of hot water owes its nomenclature to the ancient Greeks. Actually, it was Theodore Comstock who titled it in 1873. Clepsydra comes from the Greek kleptein, which means "to steal" and hydor, or

Like a twin sister to the Upper Geyser Basin, the Lower Geyser Basin is admired for its spectacular sunsets that are the fancy of landscape photographers from around the world. On the horizon, looking west, is the the rim of an ancient caldera that erupted in an epic, violent blast roughly 600,000 years ago.

"water." Together, klepsydra was a tool used to draw water and employed as a water clock in the courts of Athens. Clepsydra Geyser had its personality change abruptly in 1959 when a strong earthquake caused it to erupt continuously, sometimes throwing up a shot of water a dozen meters high.

Flanking the Lower Geyser Basin are slopes from the Madison Plateau to the west forming the Yellowstone Caldera—remnants from a catastrophic volcano that erupted 600,000 years ago. The Lower Geyser Basin is the first significant profusion of geysers that you will see while driving south from Madison Junction. An interesting footnote about the Lower Geyser Basin is that during 1877 Chief Joseph led the Nez Perce Indians through Yellowstone while trying to evade the pursing U.S. Cavalry. Part of the tribe's route follows Nez Perce Creek. During the spring, this part of the park is a busy place for elk cows which give birth to their young.Other than a brief detour through Firehole Canyon Road, you should definitely plan on taking the time to explore Fountain Flats Drive and Firehole Lake Drive. They offer a prelude to a series of geysers and a long-awaited peek at Fountain Paint Pots. In close proximity is the cluster of Spasm, Jelly , Clepsydra and several other geysers. The best time of the day for photographing geysers and hot springs is at dawn and dusk. You will feel as though you are entering another world.

The modern age has brought prospectors to Yellowstone. Although mining for gold and other minerals is illegal in the park, scientists have been probing the hot pools for microbes which have proved instrumental in developing new products. Few people who visit Yellowstone realize that the process which led to the discovery of DNA fingerprinting began here in the colorful springs of bacteria and algae.

BACTERIA DUSK

The tints which give Yellowstone's geothermal features their color are a combination of algae and bacteria. Hundreds of rare kinds of bacteria inhabit the heated pools and they belong to a family of organisms known as "protists." In recent years, biological prospectors have come to Yellowstone and harvested numerous specimens. By gleaning microbial organisms and certain enzymes, scientists have developed many new products, including the process from which DNA fingerprinting was invented. The technology gleaned from such pools has become the foundation for a $1 billion a year industry.

Although the environments you see hiking across the geyser basins may appear stark and sterile, they are rich with endemic organisms. In fact, a cup full of hot water and mud would yield thousands, if not millions, of creatures that can only be seen through the amplified power of a microscope. This is one reason why the protection of Yellowstone's geothermal wonders has taken a top priority. In addition to potentially providing the solution for a new wonder drug, the features exist as aboriginal humans first saw them. Such an unspoiled wilderness has become increasingly rare in the modern world.

Nature has set a high standard for aesthetic beauty and in America's first national park the earth and sky at sunset appear to meld into one vision. Flanking the Firehole River (left) is a rich assortment of springs that warms the chilly waters which eventually meet with the Madison River.

GREAT FOUNTAIN GEYSER and FIREHOLE SPRING

An inexplicable serenity overcomes the person who walks across a valley of geysers. Mirrored in the intricately-sculpted terraces of travertine are puffy clouds and golden sun rays. At places like Great Fountain Geyser and Firehole Spring, there is plenty of room for the mind to roam. The pace of the world almost seems to stand still for a moment, frozen in time. And then, suddenly, the geyser becomes animated. It is hard to predict when Great Fountain Geyser will next erupt but that is half the fun—allowing serendipity to be your guide. Another pond of luminous color is Firehole Spring, though it has no relation to the Firehole River. Part of the White Creek Group of geysers in the Lower Geyser Basin, gives rise to bubbling like a freshly uncorked bottle of champagne.

WATERFALLS

Hundreds of waterfalls pour through Yellowstone. Some are small and gentle, others are tall and tumble with a torrent crash that drowns out all other sound. There is a majesty to waterfalls in this park and the allure they hold for human visitors is akin to sitting on the shore of a great sea and watching the waves come rolling in. With Gibbon Falls, Firehole Falls, and Kepler Cascade, you have a trio of cataracts which carry the headwaters of major rivers. **Gibbon Falls** (below left), located between the Norris and Madison Junctions, covers a long slope which drops 84 feet from crest to toe. Eventually the current snaking through the Gibbon Canyon meets up with the Madison River. The same fate awaits the flows showering over **Firehole Falls** (below right). As the Firehole River pinches through the Firehole Canyon, it picks up speed and then drops 40 feet over the falls before sprinting again through a rocky stretch known as Firehole Cascades. The whole path can be observed from Firehole Canyon Road just south of the Madison Junction. During the springtime, all of the waterfalls in Yellowstone rumble with an added volume from melting snow. The pure, clean water that you see here is valued by human consumers hundreds of miles downstream. While Firehole Falls is situated on the lower Firehole, **Kepler Cascades** (opposite) holds primacy over upper stretches of the same river. Kepler Cascades can be reached from a parking area about 1 1/2 miles from the Old Faithful development on the route to West Thumb. Over a short span, the Firehole dips more than 100 feet. Kepler is very close to the Continental Divide which determines whether streams will flow east toward the Atlantic Ocean or west toward the Pacific. The water that spills over all three of these cataracts is headed toward the Atlantic. When winter arrives, temperatures can reach -40 degrees F, producing a sheath of ice that covers the waterfalls. It is absolutely essential that visitors stay on designated trails and not take any risks near the precipice of waterfalls because the rocks are slippery and potentially dangerous.

Water, water, everywhere. In Yellowstone the profusion of moisture translates into cascading waterfalls that tumble through primeval forests. Gibbon Falls, Firehole Falls and Kepler Cascade are all accessible to tourists traveling along the Grand Loop Road.

NORRIS GEYSER BASIN

WHIRLIGIG GEYSER

When compared to Old Faithful and the multitudes of visitors who trek across the Upper Geyser Basin, the Norris Geyser Basin seems almost deserted. By walking more than a mile (two kilometers or so) from the parking lot, you escape into a moonscape that is remembered as a pleasant surprise for most visitors who wisely take the time to stop. And listen. The topography here stands in sharp contrast to other sections of the park which are covered in either a blanket of forests or wildflower meadows. Instead, the Norris Geyser Basin seems almost spartan, abandoned, threadbare.The appearance is an illusion for residing in its vast interior is a noteworthy assembly of geysers and important pools. Prominent among them is Steamboat Geyser, the largest in the park but a feature that operates on its own schedule. Decades may pass

before its pillar of water spurts 400 feet into the sky. Then again, it may erupt today. If ever Yellowstone is to awake again with the fury of a major geologic event, Norris Geyser Basin could be its next epicenter. The ground temperatures are hottest in this basin and studies have shown that the composition of water samples collected at Norris are nearly identical to samples examined north of Yellowstone. Since the 1970s, Norris has been a valued reservoir for microbe producing hot springs and some of its enzymes are the foundation for new products and technology. After stopping at the Geyser Basin Museum, venture out into the eastern loop trail which passes by Whirlgig, Bear Den and Dark Cavern geysers. Then embark on a longer stroll through the western loop to see Steamboat , Echinus, Vixen and Porkchop geysers.

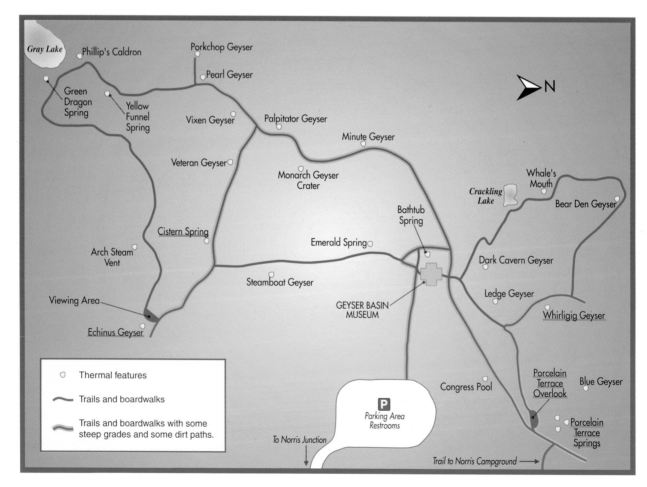

On first glance, the Norris Geyser Basin might appear to be a sprawling moonscape, but it also happens to be an extraordinary showcase for active geysers and other visual treasures. Geologists say it functions as a nursery for new hot springs. The entire complex, while less visited than the Upper Geyser Basin, is interwoven with picturesque hiking trails.

43

PORCELAIN BASIN - ECHINUS GEYSER
CISTERN SPRING

Coated by a layer of white geyserite soil, it is no mystery why this portion of the Norris geyser complex is called Porcelain Basin. As you read this sentence, the exciting story is that Porcelain Basin is a landscape in transition. New springs have sprouted within the last couple of years, indicating that change is brewing but what kind of change? No one is certain. Two features that provide solid evidence of the subterranean shift are Porcelain Terrace and Porcelain Terrace Springs. The springs quickly are being covered by a deposition of siliceous sinter. What you see today will be markedly different from what may greet your grandchildren. Hissing from the ground are sounds noises that sound like exhalations from the earth. Along the way you'll see steam vents called fumaroles and various hot springs. Meanwhile, at least some degree of short-term permanence is present at Echinus Geyser, the most predictable in the park. Echinus

comes from the Latin genus of sea urchins and the pebbles found around the geyser vent hold a resemblance to those oceanic creatures. This gusher can be seen in the Back Basin of the Norris area and eruptions have tended to occur between every half hour and 90 minutes. Back Basin is considered distinct from Porcelain Basin and indeed the ambiance is different. While Porcelain Basin is open and flat, the Back Basin is more enclosed by trees. Keep your eyes open for grizzly bears that roam across the most remote corners of the Norris area. Once you've finished at Echinus, head for Cistern Spring, which has chocolate brown and yellow shelves leading to a vat the color of the sky. Cistern Spring is growing and slowly taking over an adjacent grove of pine trees. Although the water bubbling up may appear pristine, resist the temptation to drink from it. Some of the hot springs are laced with naturally-occurring levels of arsenic.

Yellowstone has been called one of the most active geothermal hot spots on Earth and inside the stark Norris Geyser Basin the reason becomes readily apparent. After a tour of Porcelain Basin, Echinus Geyser and Cistern Spring, visitors have no doubt as to why the United Nations has declared Yellowstone to be a place worth preserving for all time.

MAMMOTH HOT SPRINGS

MINERVA TERRACE

In the slopes that rise above Mammoth Hot Springs—the administrative headquarters of Yellowstone— a stylized tier of mineralized rock formations move incrementally downhill almost as if they were deliberately set in motion by the hand of a human sculptor. In fact, nature has been active here for thousands of years and the creative medium is hot spring water. Each day, drip by drip, new shelves of travertine emerge at places like Minerva Terrace, named after the Roman goddess of artists and sculptors. It is all part of a larger complex of hot springs which comprise the entire Mammoth Hot Springs area. Mammoth Hot Springs has a completely different variety of geothermal features than are found elsewhere in the park. You won't find geysers, but you will see the methodical system by which the terraces were born, and still growing. The expansion of Minerva Terrace is fueled by mineral-rich water amorphously spilling out of Minerva Spring. Some of the travertine textures resemble icicles while others give the impression of fast-moving streams even though they are complete stationary. Although liquid is the substance that shaped the tiers, the staircases are solid rock. Along with Jupiter, Opal and Orange springs, Minerva Terrace has been among the most active. For several years after Yellowstone was created in 1872, Mammoth Hot Springs was the base camp for soldiers with the U.S. Cavalry. The vintage stone buildings that you see, including the Park Visitor Center, owe their origins to this period. Among the other inhabitants at Mammoth is a herd of elk that frequently lounge and graze on the lawns. In the late summer and early autumn, Mammoth comes alive when bull elk (male animals with horns) begin challenging one another for the right to breed with females. At this time, bull elk emit trumpet-like calls in a ritual known as "bugling."

The terraces of travertine at Mammoth Hot Springs contain a form of natural perfection that could not have come from human hands. Elegant, yet rough and unpolished,these natural sculptures are crafted slowly, drop by drop, over thousands of years.

CANARY SPRING

Side by side, two expressions of calcified aqua march down the slopes of Mammoth Hot Spring—terraces forged of travertine, and bulbous rock cascades resembling frozen waterfalls. At Canary Spring sprawling across the Main Terrace, water seeps out from a pool at the top of a spring and descends a staircase laden with colorful algae and bacteria. Where the angle of the dripping water is too steep, a slippery slope forms and drops almost 100 meters. Canary Spring was given its avian name even before it officially appeared on tourist maps in 1904. The feature does not resemble a bird, however, except in its ruddy yellow coloration, the result of specialized bacteria clinging to the deposition of of sulfur. This spring can be explored via a footpath that begins close to the Mammoth Hotel and climbs well above the site of what used to be historic Fort Yellowstone. The feature seems perpetually covered by a veil of steam. Geologists say that Canary Spring is very active and slowly migrating across the hill beneath it. Above Canary Spring is the enchanting wonderland of the Upper Terrace. It is so "otherwordly" in its appearance that during the late 1970s the producers of the Star Trek movies wanted to use it as a backdrop for the planet Vulcan. A few miles to the north of Yellowstone on the way to the old mining town of Jardine, there is evidence of another hot spring complex that was active in previous millennia. Like the geyser basins around Old Faithful, the hot springs at Mammoth are always in a state of flux. Located in one section of the Upper Terrace is a cave known as Devil's Kitchen that was formed by a now-extinct hot spring. Early in the 20th century, tourists used to explore the cave but in 1939 the Park Service shut down the explorations because of carbon dioxide gasses. Together, all the springs in the Mammoth area spew out about two tons of escaping travertine (calcium carbonate) limestone every day and discharge 500 gallons every minute. The material is different from the geyserite found in the geyser basins, which is made of silicon dioxide.

A surreal white glow appears to emanate from Canary Spring, one of the more spectacular features in the Mammoth Hot Springs area. The glistening headwalls are made of mineralized water called travertine, which percolates to the surface from deep in the ground.

Mammoth Hotel is the rustic hub of visitor activity in the northern region of Yellowstone and it provides an ideal base camp from which visits can be planned to Petrified Tree and Roaring Mountain. It also provides easy access to several travertine terraces and is only a close distance away from Liberty Cap, the skeleton of an ancient hot spring which is now extinct.

MAMMOTH HOTEL

The hotel you see (upper left) at Mammoth Hot Springs today, while rustic and cozy, is not the same one that greeted tourists at the turn of the century. The third major hotel to operate at Mammoth, this one was constructed during the Great Depression between 1936 and 1937. In the early days of Yellowstone's history, tourists were ferried to the old hotel by stagecoach and then, with the arrival of the automobile, by various versions of motorcar. A sizeable number of foreign visitors explore the park in tour busses and stay at the modern Mammoth Hotel which has 94 rooms inside its stately structure (more than 100 cabins also are tucked out behind it).

LIBERTY CAP

In addition to the hot springs, another prominent symbol of the Mammoth area is the stone silhouette of Liberty Cap (lower left). Rising 37 feet high, Liberty Cap is the travertine cone of a hot spring thought to be 2,500 years old. The cone was named by park explorer Ferdinand Hayden who suggested that the top of Liberty Cap resembled the hats worn by soldiers during the French Revolution.

PETRIFIED TREE

East of Mammoth Hot Springs just before you arrive at Roosevelt-Tower Junction there is a turnoff that leads to Petrified Tree (below left). At one point, there used to be two petrified trees standing here but vandalism led to the dismantling of one ancient stump and the contraction of a fence around the other. If you want to see the remnants of a complete petrified forest, it can be viewed on the high ramparts of Specimen Ridge overlooking the Lamar Valley.

ROARING MOUNTAIN

Along the way to Petrified Tree, you will notice the beginnings of a new forest. In 1988, forest fires swept across 793,880 acres (321,272 hectares) of Yellowstone, or about 36 percent of its land mass. South of Mammoth Hot Springs on the road to Norris Junction is a barren mountain slope called Roaring Mountain. Roaring Mountain resembles the side of a an active volcano. The vents of steam you see are fumaroles of escaping gas.

Called one of the prettiest waterfalls in Yellowstone, Tower Fall spills over a ledge of rhyolite and sets adjacent to the famous Grand Canyon of the Yellowstone.

TOWER FALL

Tumbling 132 feet over a humbling rock ledge, Tower Fall ranks as one of the most spectacular cascades in all of Yellowstone. Situated along the Grand Loop Road between Roosevelt and Canyon Village, this waterfall is a popular destination for painters and photographers. Upstream from the falls along the banks of Tower Creek, the water gains momentum and crashes down through pillars of smooth rhyolite. Then it pours over the precipice and enters a small canyon which leads to the much larger Grand Canyon of the Yellowstone River. Tourists are afforded breathtaking views of the waterfall from above and below from a short hiking trail that winds to the bottom. In the early 1870s, watercolor painter Thomas Moran spent several days at Tower Fall, making sketches that eventually were turned into large paintings and presented before the Congress of the United States. The artist's renderings so inspired lawmakers that in 1872, President Ulysses S Grant set aside Yellowstone forever as a place for people to recreate.

GRAND CANYON OF THE YELLOWSTONE

There is no way tourists can prepare themselves for the Grand Canyon of the Yellowstone because it seems to emerge suddenly, without warning, and then serves up a feast for the eyes. Stretching 4,000 feet across and 24 miles long, the gorge plummets between 800 and 1,200 feet (366 m) from the rim to the Yellowstone River which snakes along its floor. Accented by eroding cliffs of yellow and red rhyolite, the color of the canyon changes with the shifting angle of the sun. The view is apt to leave you speechless, just as it has millions of people who have stood here before. Although its name was inspired by the Grand Canyon in Arizona, this riverine chasm has its own majesty. If you look closely, seven distinct layers of geologic history are written in the walls, including breccia formed by ancient volcanic ash, sediments from when the park was covered by an inland sea, and gouges left behind by glaciers. Hiking trails actually dip inside the canyon walls and expose the ears to the river's roar below.

The best views of the canyon come from both the north and south rims but start your journey at Canyon Village, which has restaurants, cabins, and campgrounds, and then take the one-way North Rim Drive.

At night, National Park Service rangers offer free talks at the Canyon Village amphitheater about the local natural history and wildlife in the area.

The chasm of the Grand Canyon of the Yellowstone is simply overwhelming. Ever present is the roar of the Yellowstone River and the crashing of two great cascades, the Upper and Lower falls.

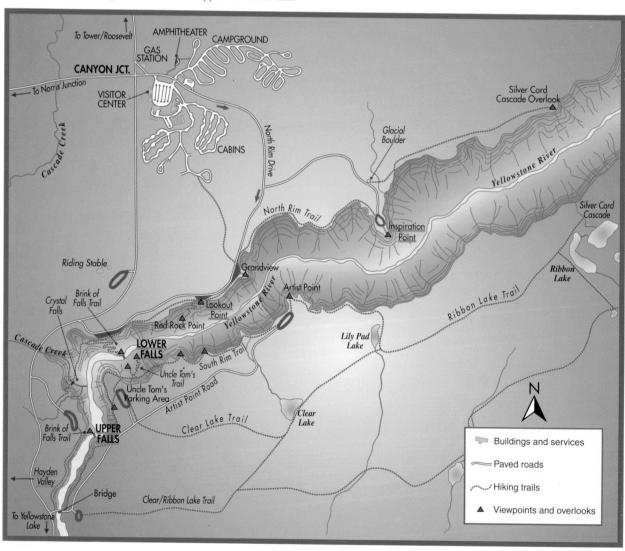

INSPIRATION POINT and LOOKOUT POINT

Protruding into the maw of the Grand Canyon of the Yellowstone, both Inspiration Point and Lookout Point offer the best perches for spying the gorge from the North Rim. Inspiration Point is accessible from North Rim Drive and offers extraordinary sunset views. Over hundreds of thousands of years, the Yellowstone River has eaten its way deeper into the canyon, causing the soft walls to erode. The different hues of color come from rhyolite which is tinged with iron oxide. A variety of animal life calls the canyon home, including occasionally-sighted bald eagles and osprey which swoop toward the river and pull trout from the water. You may even see an osprey nest built upon the top of a remote spire in the canyon. The most common avian inhabitants, however, are big black ravens that nest in pine trees nearby, and ground squirrels. An excellent hiking trail begins at the glacial boulder near the Inspiration Point parking lot and leads to a place called Seven Mile Hole. This trip requires a full day in and a full day out, as well as a camping permit. Further along on the North Rim Drive is the trail to Lookout Point, where you can see the Lower Falls far off in the distance. Most enticing perhaps is the stunning sheer cliff that drops to the river's edge. The Yellowstone River is one of the wildest free-flowing streams in the lower 48 states. It is dangerous and illegal to hike off trail so don't even consider it. Rather, relax and enjoy the scenery. Across the canyon, you will be able to spot other tourists gathered at Artist's Point on the South Rim. The view of the Lower Falls from Artist's Point and Lookout Point are among the most photographed in the national parks. Be forewarned: Conditions in the canyon often are breezy, and temperatures tend to be much cooler so bring a jacket as well as your camera.

Two of the premier overlooks for gazing to the Grand Canyon of the Yellowstone are Inspiration Point and Lookout Point which afford a bird's eye view. Both are perched on the north side of the gorge and accessible via Canyon Village.

To many connoisseurs of natural aesthetics, the Lower Falls represent the loveliest cascade in North America. Thundering into the Grand Canyon of the Yellowstone, they are framed by the golden walls of the gorge. They are higher even than the famous cataracts of Niagara in New York and Canada.

LOWER FALLS

Few sights are more profound than that of the Lower Falls in the Grand Canyon of the Yellowstone. As the highest waterfall in the park (308 feet), it rages into the gorge with tremendous power and symbolizes the ruggedness that defines the canyon for the next 24 miles. When melting snow swells the Yellowstone River, 63,500 gallons of water per second spill over the falls, creating a roar that resounds miles away. By comparison, fewer than 6,000 gallons per second pass over the threshold in late autumn at low water. Visitors can attain an intimate glimpse of the falls by hiking the Brink-of-the-Falls Trail which descends via a series of switchbacks to the lip of the Lower Falls.Up close, the color of the water appears green, and as it leaps into the void of the canyon below, rainbows often appear in the mist. The Lower Falls are a few times higher than the famous cascades as Niagara in New York and Canada. The canyon has the ambiance of vacuous outdoor cathedral that is as mesmerizing as watching the waves come in from the ocean. Water has rained over the falls for millennia upon millennia.

ARTIST POINT
and UPPER FALLS

Some of the finest landscape painters in America have celebrated the Grand Canyon of the Yellowstone on canvass, including Albert Bierstadt, Thomas Moran and Lucien Powell. Each of them set up their easels at Artist's Point and then felt incapable of conveying the grandeur. The paintings they made, nonetheless, are on display in the country's most prestigious museums.

Artist's Point is certainly a premier vantage from which to witness the Lower Falls, but another promenade is "Uncle Tom's" also located on the South Rim. To get there, travel southward after you leave the North Rim Drive, and follow the signs to Artist's Point but stop at the Uncle Tom's Parking Area. If you want to stretch your legs, consider a brief walk on the South Rim Trail between Uncle Tom's and Artist's Point. Another option is to descend toward the Uncle Tom's viewing area in front of the Lower Falls. A place so close to the falls that you can almost taste them, this viewpoint is named after Uncle Tom Richardson who served as an early tourist guide and cleared this first trail to the river. As you drive back to the Grand Loop Road, don't forget to stop at the Upper Falls. Most tourists fail to realize that there are actually two waterfalls on the Yellowstone River just above the Grand Canyon. The Upper Falls dip 109 feet and spill into a gentle pool. Less than half a mile later (0.8km), the river dives again at the Lower Falls.

It is impossible to make a bad photograph from the prominent overlook at Artist Point. Here, the river and the golden spires of rhyolite pull the eye and the camera lens toward the Lower Falls. Just upstream (below) is another waterfall, the Upper Falls, that is smaller but no less pleasant to gaze upon.

HAYDEN VALLEY

Hayden Valley is the placid heart of Yellowstone because it has a little bit of everything. Its meadows go on and on, for as far as the eye can see. Mountains rise in relief, and the sky looms large with puffy pillows of cumulus clouds and summer storms. Hayden Valley is named after Ferdinand Hayden who led three surveys of the park on behalf of the government in 1871, 1872, and 1878. It was said that during the eruption of geysers, the veteran explorer would be moved to tears. Hayden loved the park landscape and found many things that brought joy to his face in the picturesque dell. Traveling across this rolling, treeless plain is akin to going back in time. Actually, Hayden Valley isn't a plain but the floor of the ancient Yellowstone Caldera. On a typical spring, summer, or early autumn day, tourists in Hayden Valley will be able to count hundreds of bison scattered in a massive herd. The behemoths, which can weigh as much as one ton, assemble here to graze upon the profusion of grasses and cool themselves during the hottest

months in the Yellowstone River. Striking a sharp contrast to the river that thunders through the Grand Canyon of the Yellowstone, the waterway is wide, pastoral and slow-moving. It is a magnet for wildlife. By the end of June, buffalo mothers in Hayden Valley have given birth to calves and set out in distinctive nursery bands to rear the young. Meanwhile, bison bulls wander off by themselves in search of solitude. In August, bulls challenge one another in displays of dominance and then breed with willing females. Bison are exciting to watch, but the animals that make Hayden Valley seem truly wild is the presence of grizzly bears, the most fearsome predators in the park. Grizzlies regularly are sighted in the early morning and late evening hours. Other animals of note are dozens of species of songbirds, hawks and falcons, white pelicans, geese and ducks, bald eagles, river otters and beaver. While Hayden Valley is a paradise for wildlife lovers in the summer, it turns brutally cold and lonely in winter.

Hayden Valley is the pastoral heart of Yellowstone and here visitors find great herds of bison lumbering across the high mountain prairie. A magnet for water birds, otters, and trumpeter swans, the Yellowstone River is Hayden Valley's main water artery. The placid river cuts a wide circuitous path which ultimately leads to the Grand Canyon of the Yellowstone.

YELLOWSTONE LAKE

Clear, ice cold, and cobalt blue, Yellowstone Lake is one of the largest mountain lakes in the world. In many ways, it is the aquatic counterpart to Hayden Valley and indeed both are connected through the course of the Yellowstone River. Rimmed by 110 miles (177km) of shoreline, the dimensions of this spacious tarn are impressive as you gaze across its surface toward high, snow-crowned mountains. The body of water itself is 20 miles long and 14 miles wide (32 X 23 km) but what speaks to its allure are not statistics but pure natural aesthetics. You will find buffalo munching grasses on Yellowstone Lake's northern shore, watch bald eagles sailing aloft in search of trout near the marina at Bridge Bay, and delight at river otters maneuvering in and out of the geothermal coves at West Thumb. There is plenty of terrain to explore, especially if you like boating and fishing. The lake is a biological reservoir for Yellowstone's famous populations of cutthroat trout and it also attracts a sizeable colony of white pelicans that congregate near its outlet at Fishing Bridge. The lake expresses itself through a variety of moods. Although the open water can appear calm and tranquil on a sunny day, an afternoon breeze can turn it perilous for canoeists who are unprepared. That's why many visitors elect to take guided tours and fishing trips which originate at Bridge Bay. Yellowstone Lake is very deep in spots—up to 390 feet (120 m)— and the muddy lake bed is home to a variety of geothermal phenomena.

Modern explorers have sent miniature, remote-controlled submarines to the bottom of the lake to examine the volatile steam vents and underground geysers. What they discovered was a cadre of organisms usually found in the deep trenches of the ocean. While several streams feed into the lake, the Yellowstone River starts at the southern end of this freshwater sea and departs from the northern shore on a journey that will take it hundreds of miles toward an eventual rendezvous with the Missouri River in the state of North Dakota.

Yellowstone Lake is one of the largest high-altitude bodies of fresh water in the world. Snow-capped peaks tower over the cold depths which hold plentiful populations of native cutthroat trout. Bison often can be seen grazing in the grassy meadows.

*The Lake Hotel is the grand old mother of overnight
accommodations in Yellowstone. The oldest standing hotel in the
park, it sits on the northern shore of Yellowstone Lake and exudes
an ambiance that takes visitors back to the 19th century.*

LAKE HOTEL

Fronting the north shore of Yellowstone Lake is a massive yellow edifice that architecturally conveys the elegance of neo-classicism and the gothic charm of the old West. The oldest hotel in the park, Lake Hotel carries with it a steeped tradition. Built between 1889 and 1891, it is a monument to the past. Like the Old Faithful Inn, this vintage guest lodge dates back to an era when national parks were just a new idea and overnight accommodations were designed to be as magnificent as the scenery around them. Many decades ago, the hotel was part of the "Grand Circuit" which included stops at Old Faithful Inn, the Canyon Hotel, Roosevelt Lodge and Mammoth Hotel. Exploring the park then was done in the carriage of a stagecoach and demanded at least a week.

After spending all day out in the wilds, hotel guests were treated to savory meals, evening entertainment and feathery beds. The tradition still continues today. A favorite pastime of tourists at Lake Hotel is to sit in the reading room before and after dinner sipping a beverage refreshment and watching the sun set or storms gather over the seemingly interminable surface of the tarn. It makes for wonderful natural drama. Here, the lobby of the hotel is filled with music from either the resident pianist or visiting musicians. Young and old gather on comfortable furniture which is spread across a shiny wooden floor and encircled by large windows. Over the years a variety of celebrities have stayed at the Lake Hotel—from Presidents to European royalty. The appeal of Lake Hotel is that it attracts families as well as the rich and famous because its rates are reasonably priced. Rooms must be reserved well in advance of your visit, however, because it is one of the most popular hotels in the park. If you can't find a room here, consider booking a motel room just down the road at the less-expensive Lake Lodge. Both facilities, which combined have 296 rooms and cabins, offer spectacular views of the lake and there are several hiking trails nearby that are easy to explore. Lake Lodge itself is an impressive, rustic structure that still carries with it scents of lodgepole pine. Bison are often spotted lumbering through the meadows and, in springtime, grizzly bears fish for trout in the streams.

MUD VOLCANO

Between Hayden Valley and Yellowstone Lake along the Grand Loop, motorists come to a curve in the road and discover balloons of gaseous clouds lifting into the sky. You have just reached the entrance to Mud Volcano, another example of Yellowstone's strange geothermal phenomena. Mud Volcano isn't like a real volcano in the classic sense of the word. For one thing, there isn't a giant cone emitting lava, and for another real volcanoes tend to be much bigger in size as evidenced by the epic Yellowstone Caldera that blew a hole in the landscape many kilometers in diameter

roughly 600,000 years ago. Instead, Mud Volcano is a fascinating series of mud vents that share a deep connection with the fiery belly of the earth. Similar to the geysers, hot springs, and fumaroles, the mud pots here are created and maintained by escaping heat Leaving your car and hiking along the boardwalk trails, the first sensation that greets you is the pungent odor of sulfur and the sounds of churning lava rock. One of the most popular attractions is Dragon's Mouth where it sounds as if the ground is actually breathing.

Mud Volcano, located between Fishing Bridge and Hayden Valley, is home to a curious collection of hissing, gurgling vents and sulfurous plumes of steam. It provides yet another example of Yellowstone's 10,000 geothermal features, which, in sheer number, represents more than are found in the rest of the world combined.

WEST THUMB

At West Thumb, hot springs are wedded to the sandy shoreline of Yellowstone Lake. Scattered along this sloping beachhead is a string of joyous pools that geologists say bear remarkable similarities with the phenomena around Old Faithful and the west side of the park several miles (kilometers) away. The boardwalks at West Thumb give travelers a compelling excuse to stretch the feet as you tour the Grand Loop Road. West Thumb takes its name from a large bay on the southwestern corner of Yellowstone Lake. The emerald-colored hot springs appear to rise out of nowhere. They are tropical gems in a landscape which is chilly and windblown. One of the most vibrant attractions is Thumb Paint Pots that shines in an array of pastels. Keeping company with this lonely group of hot springs are geysers in the West Thumb Geyser Basin. Over the past century, the temperatures at several pools and geysers in the vicinity of West Thumb have fluctuated dramatically following earthquakes. It is a telltale sign that under the placid surface is complicated network of vents and fissures. Many of these features, in fact, are kindred to those found north of Old Faithful. The scene at West Thumb should also give you an idea of the type of geothermal activity that exists in Yellowstone Lake. Submerged on the bottom is a kingdom of hot water seeps. During the winter, river otters often are seen running across the ice-covered surface of the lake at West Thumb and diving into circles of open water

A kindred cousin to the geyser fields found around Old Faithful, the Old Thumb area is located on the southwest shore of Yellowstone Lake and is known for its abundance of radiant hot springs.

Typical of the soothing pools is Abyss Pool that bubbles with boiling water and azure color.

ABYSS POOL

Abyss Pool is exactly what its name implies: a wellspring of extremely hot water that dips into an abyss of color. Located at West Thumb near the icy waters of Yellowstone Lake, this steamy aquamarine bowl is as pretty as any in the park. As water spills out onto the brittle lid of crust surrounding it, the run-off travels downhill toward the shore of Yellowstone Lake. In this shallow channel are rocks covered with brown-orange bacteria and pods of floating algae. Abyss Pool has lured tourists for more than a century. Although it is a well-known fixture in the West Thumb Geyser Basin, this hot spring was not named until 1935. Compared to the Old Faithful area, West Thumb receives only a fraction of the visitors, which is why it makes such an ideal location to picnic. Down the road from West Thumb a short distance is the developed area of Grant Village where there is a campground, gift shops, restaurant and ranger station, all on the southern shore of Yellowstone Lake.

BLACK POOL
and FISHING CONE

Among the oddities located in the West Thumb Geyser Basin, two of the more curious features are Black Pool, which has clear, blue-colored water, and Fishing Cone. Black Pool, like other springs in the park, is home to millions of tiny micro-organisms which are specially adapted to live in boiling water. Although Black Pool is larger, Fishing Cone became a famous stop in the 19th century. At this spot, fishermen would catch trout from Yellowstone Lake and then lower the fish into the boiling water to cook them. Thousands of tourists performed this ritual and it was only after this method of cooking fish was questioned by health officials that it was prohibited. Today, visitors are encouraged to photograph the tiny knob of rock from a distance. While Fishing Cone appears to be a docile hot spring, don't be fooled. It is actually a dormant geyser that at various times has erupted with a fury. In 1921, a fisherman there was burned by the hot water.

Black Pool is surrounded by an orange-brown palette of color that contains millions of micro-organisms that have learned to survive in water that is hostile to most other life forms. Although Fishing Cone appears docile, it is actually a semi-active geyser cone. Earlier in the 20th century, park visitors cooked fish in the natural pot but today the practice is prohibited.

GRAND TETON
NATIONAL PARK

When it comes to describing the sheer majesty of Wyoming's Teton Mountains, words alone are insufficient. Dappled by snow, pointing like buffalo horns into the sky, the Tetons are instantly recognizable and yet attainable physically only by the agile determination of a rock climber.
Rising more than 7,000 feet (2,134 m) straight up from the valley floor of Jackson Hole, this jagged wall of granite symbolizes everything a mountain should be.
While the tall peaks are the prominent focal points of Grand Teton National Park the summits themselves comprise merely a portion of the park's total land mass. Located south of Yellowstone, Grand Teton Park has its own ambiance which is very different from its larger and more famous neighbor. Yellowstone's natural wonders, while fantastic, are subtle and passive by comparison. In Grand Teton, the beauty is almost overwhelming. The genesis of Grand Teton began in 1929 when a smaller version of today's preserve was set aside, through the park gradually has expanded to its current size of 310,000 acres (1,256 square kilometers). Only one-seventh as big as Yellowstone, it is still easy nonetheless to escape the crowds and relish in solitude. For more than a century, the environs around Grand Teton and Jackson Hole have been the domain of authentic cowboys pushing herds of cattle onto the open range. If the Tetons look familiar it may be because they are one of the most photographed mountain ranges in the world, or perhaps because they also have been adored by Hollywood. The classic Western movie, Shane, used Grand Teton as its setting and today you still can see wranglers riding horses at local dude ranches. It is this maverick spirit that fills the hearts of all who enter the park. Besides excellent wildlife watching opportunities, visitors can whet their thirst for adventure by climbing to alpine summits, floating in a raft down the Snake River, renting a canoe and paddling through a chain of lakes, or simply relaxing with a picnic lunch at a favorite promontory. The first destination for any park guest should be the Visitor Center in Moose where you can become acquainted with all the options. Park rangers are very helpful with pointing out things to do and see. There are three primary roads to keep in mind: (1) The main highway (Highway 89) that runs parallel to the mountains and covers the entire length of the park from the town of Jackson, Wyoming to the southern entrance of Yellowstone; (2) The 42-mile scenic Teton Park Loop Road (which should not be missed!) that takes visitors within reach of hiking trails and lakes at the base of the Tetons; and (3) The Antelope Flats/Gros Ventre Loop that also is quite picturesque and introduces visitors to the quaint little town of Kelly. A fourth option, if you have the time, is the secluded Moose-Wilson Road, that lights up in September with an explosion of leaves changing color on the trees.

GRAND TETON

"TETONS"

Wherever you go in Grand Teton National Park, the lofty profile of the Tetons is never very far away. Revered by mountaineers as a challenging alpine paradise, these peaks attract the finest climbers in the world. Highest among them is the Grand Teton at 13,770 feet (4,197 m). The most difficult routes up this landmark still rank as a coveted prize for those who are willing to take risks. Together with the Grand, Teewinot Mountain at 12,325 feet and Mount Owen at 12,928 feet form what is called "The Cathedral Group." All you need to do is take a look at their silhouettes to understand why the Tetons elicit instant comparisons to the Alps of Europe. While three peaks are indeed prominent, the range is studded by many summits. Their pyramid-shaped lines give them the appearance of three mighty steeples. The name of the Tetons, however, has its origins in a less dignified observation. Early in the 19th century, French-Canadian fur trappers who were trying to catch beaver on the western slope of the mountains gazed at the other side of the three peaks and called them "Les Trois Tetons" or more simply, "the three breasts." Tetons have been part of the American vocabulary ever since.

The closer one gets to these mountains, the more hypnotic they become. Seven of the Teton pinnacles exceed 3,600 meters (12,000 feet). To get to the top of the Grand does not demand years of specialized mountaineering training . There are a few climbing schools located in the park that offer tourists instruction in how to ascend the easiest routes with a guide. Approximately 9,000 people climb some portion of the Tetons each year and thousands more go hiking on established trails. Flanking the Cathedral Group to the north (to the right as you look at the Tetons from Jackson Hole) are Storm Point, Symmetry Spire, Mount St. John, Rockchuck Peak, and Mount

The highlight of any trip to Grand Teton National Park is the opportunity to see the Teton Mountains in all their glory. There are many travelers who refer to them as "the Alps of the American West."

The tallest of the Teton peaks is the Grand Teton but this summit shares its throne with several other towering points of granite. When viewed from the flats of Jackson Hole, the Tetons strike a rugged silhouette. These slopes represent a Mecca for mountain climbers. As the first morning light basks the Tetons in alpenglow (following pages) the moon has begun its slow descent to mark the end of night.

While summer is the busiest time in Grand Teton National Park, winter gives the landscape a special glaze of grandeur. In the calm before an approaching winter storm, the Tetons under a mantle of snow are breathtaking and serene.

Moran, which has a flat top. During the summer, you can see the remains of the "Skillet Glacier" on Mount Moran which has the outline of a frying pan. The ice dates back perhaps 4,000 years and has taken the place of massive glacial shields that covered the mountain during the Pleistocene Ice Age. Within Grand Teton National Park, there is an elite team of climbing rangers who rescue and assist modern explorers who run into trouble. The first unofficial ascent of the Grand Teton reportedly was made in 1872 by James Stevenson and Nathaniel Langford. In 1924, Geraldine Lucas became the first woman to reach the summit. Interestingly, she was 59 years old when she accomplished the memorable feat.

Winter bestows a regal luster upon the ramparts of Grand Teton National Park. At the highest elevations, snowfall piles up in the mountains many feet (meters) deep. Prior to the arrival of European settlers, neither Indians nor fur trappers resided in Jackson Hole permanently. The reason was the long winter when game became scarce. While heavy snow may have been a bane to the

first explorers, today it is a bonus for alpine and nordic skiers who treat the region as a sporting Mecca. The Jackson Hole Ski Area was constructed across a portion of the Teton's eastern face but it lies just outside the park boundary. For the most part, winter is a quiet, solemn time in Grand Teton. Bears are fast asleep in their underground dens, the lakes are frozen over, and the interior park highway is closed. The snowy months give local residents an opportunity to reflect upon the magic of Grand Teton. Said one woman who has lived in Jackson Hole for 50 years: "I've seen the Alps, climbed in the Himalayas, and visited the mountains of South America. But the Tetons are special because they resonate with soul. After you see them once, you can travel thousands of miles away but you will never forget them." The Snake River Overlook (above) is a hallowed setting for nature photographers in the U.S. Popularized by legendary American landscape photographer Ansel Adams, this winter scene brings together all of the critical elements to create a memorable portrait: The moodiness of an approaching storm over the Tetons; the last fingers of sunlight fading in the west, and a coating of snow and ice on the Snake River in the foreground. At night during the winter, traces of the Northern Lights flash across the heavens as the clear cold skies emit a brilliant luminescence. Star gazers delight at the prospects. Even in the grip of winter, the mountains call out profoundly to climbers. On New Year's Day each year, a hardy group of alpinists make a pilgrimage to the top of the Grand Teton as a greeting of goodwill.

In the span of 7,000 feet (2,100 meters) conditions can radically change in the mountains. The valley floor of Jackson Hole might be green and abloom with wildflowers while the tip of the Tetons may be socked in by clouds and blizzards. The rule of the backcountry is to always be prepared for adverse weather. Every month of the year park visitors have awoke to snowfall in the mountains. From December until March (photograph below) park rangers lead skiing trips and snowshoeing adventures into the park interior from trailheads ordinarily used by hikers. Daytime temperatures in the winter typically range from -25 degrees to 50 degrees F (-31 degrees to 10 degrees C). Humans are joined by other intrepid animals. The dizzying crags of the mountains are home to bighorn sheep and raptors which nest in the remote cliffs. According to one alpinist, coyote tracks were found in the dead of winter on a few of the tallest peaks indicating that *Homo sapiens* is not alone in its quest to reach the top of the park.

After heavy snows bury the hiking trails, skiers and snowshoers waste little time in exploring the park backcountry. Snow has fallen upon the Tetons in every month of the year. Captured in a masterpiece of symmetry, the Tetons (following pages) cast their reflection upon the glassy surface of the Snake River.

SNAKE RIVER

Birthed from the southern mountains of
Yellowstone, the headwaters of the Snake River
are pure and pristine. Never was there a river
with a more breathtaking setting in America. As
the Snake winds through Grand Teton it first
enters Jackson Lake and then cuts a meandering
course southward across the entire valley. It is a
very important channel of water which eventually
joins the mighty Columbia River. About 40 miles
(65 kilometers) of the Snake flow through the
park. In Grand Teton, it is a lifeline for wildlife
populations and it nurtures the landscape.
Downstream, it is a source of water for cities and
farmers, including the famous potato fields of
Idaho. One of the more bucolic sections of the
Snake is the Oxbow Bend where moose, bald
eagles and an assortment of other wildlife species
gather around the slow-moving current. The
Snake also is highly regarded by fishermen and
floaters. Of the 17 species of fish found in Grand
Teton Park, the most coveted by sport anglers is
the native Snake River cutthroat trout which are
common in the river.

*The Snake River is considered a biological lifeline for many
different species of plants and animals. Few rivers in the U.S. have
a more spectacular setting which makes this aqua serpent a
popular playground for boaters and fishermen.*

HISTORIC PLACES

Human history in Grand Teton National Park is often as fascinating as the wonders of nature. Jackson Hole as a term originated in 1829 when William Sublette named the dell beneath the Tetons after his fur trapper friend David Jackson who hunted and fished in he area. Jackson was not the only intrepid mountain man. Two others, perhaps better known, were John Colter and Jim Bridger. In the parlance of maintain men, the word "hole" was substituted for "valley." Jackson, Bridger, Colter, and Sublette were nomads with no permanent home. The first settlers of European ancestry to stay in Jackson Hole year-round probably came in 1884. Three years later Pierce and Margaret Cunningham arrived and built a **cabin** (below) that can be seen off the main park highway just north and across the road from the Triangle X dude ranch.

Before there were permanent bridges built across the Snake River, getting from one side of the park to the other could be tricky (and wet!) if you weren't careful. When Bill Menor came to Jackson Hole in 1894, he saw the vexing problem as an opportunity for commercial gain. Erecting a **ferry** (lower left) that used cables strung across the river, he charged travelers a fee to be carried from one side of the Snake to the other. Today at the old Menor Ferry and homestead near Moose, you will also find the cabin that belonged to pioneer Maude Noble. In 1923, Noble's home became a historic meeting place for it was here that the idea for Grand Teton Park was first discussed. Today, visitors can walk along a self-guided nature trail. While there are many who say the grandeur of Grand Teton makes them feel closer to God, the **Chapel of the Transfiguration** (upper left) is a place where religious ceremonies happen routinely during the summer. The tiny log chapel, which sits in close proximity to Menor's Ferry and the Noble cabin, was built in 1925 by pioneers who wanted to have their own place of worship. The building is open to travelers and regular Episcopalian church services are held every Sunday during the summer in addition to weddings.

Dispersed throughout the park are buildings and other reminders of the first pioneers who came to Jackson Hole in the 1880s.

JACKSON LAKE and JENNY LAKE

Pressed up against the foot of the Teton Range, Jackson Lake and Jenny Lake are two sparkling rubies which have a magnetic effect on park visitors. These are piedmont lakes, which means their deep beds were gouged by glaciers moving across the valley. The biggest tarn in Grand Teton Park, Jackson Lake is the first major body of water you encounter while driving south from Yellowstone. Some of the oldest archeological artifacts were collected along its shores, indicating that native peoples hunted and camped here during the summers for 12,000 years. The outlet of Jackson Lake is the Snake River and water levels are controlled by a dam on the southeast shore. Jackson Lake, named after 19th century fur trapper David Jackson, is popular among recreationists year around. During the summer months, wind surfers in wet suits glide over the cold surface and fishermen go searching for massive lake trout. In winter, anglers return and fish through the ice. At Jackson Lake Lodge, hotel guests are treated to a spectacular view of the Tetons and there are trail rides on horseback that set out every morning and afternoon. Further south, Jenny Lake turns frenetic with human activity during the summer and offers one of the prettiest views in the park. Jenny Lake was named after the daughter of an early Jackson Hole pioneer. Although it is only a mile across, the green-blue water leaves a much bigger impression on the mind because the Tetons literally tower above it. For a small fee, visitors can take a boat ride across the lake form the main parking area, and then walk to Hidden Falls which cascade through an enchanting forest. This path leading from the boat dock also connects with the Cascade Canyon Trail, the most popular in the park. Jenny Lake is the base camp for one of the climbing schools located in Grand Teton and the cliffs rising above Hidden Falls are a training area for novice mountaineers. Besides a rustic, four-star hotel located on the northern shore of the lake, there is a campground at Jenny Lake but spaces fill up quick and it is recommended that you arrive at the ranger station early in the day to reserve a place to pitch your tent. While touring the park via the Teton Park Loop Road, don't forget five other lakes which are equally dramatic. String, Leigh, Bradley and Taggart lakes each have a trail leading to them and offer seclusion that you won't find at Jenny.

A necklace of glacial-carved lakes are strung along the base of the Tetons. Jackson Lake and Jenny Lake are two piedmont tarns that are symbols of the park's tranquility.

There is an expression in Grand Teton National Park: If you don't like the weather, just wait a while because it is certain to change. No matter what the season, the park is always a place of natural drama.

JACKSON HOLE

The town of Jackson is a busy hub for entertainment in Jackson Hole. Calling itself "the last and best of the Old West," this small community of a few thousand residents has a wide selection of shops, restaurants and theaters to fill your night after a long day of exploring nearby Grand Teton National Park. Perhaps best known is the legendary **Million Dollar Cowboy Bar** where patrons can sit in a real saddle and dance to authentic cowboy music. Across the street from the Cowboy Bar is the **Jackson Town Square**—a small park—that is ornamented by four **elkhorn arches**. The gateways are constructed of real antlers that are shed each year by male elk on the National Elk Refuge.

The town of Jackson is the busy gateway to Grand Teton National Park and the big valley of Jackson Hole. There is a variety of things to do and see, including a famous Old West shootout that occurs every evening around the Jackson Town Square.

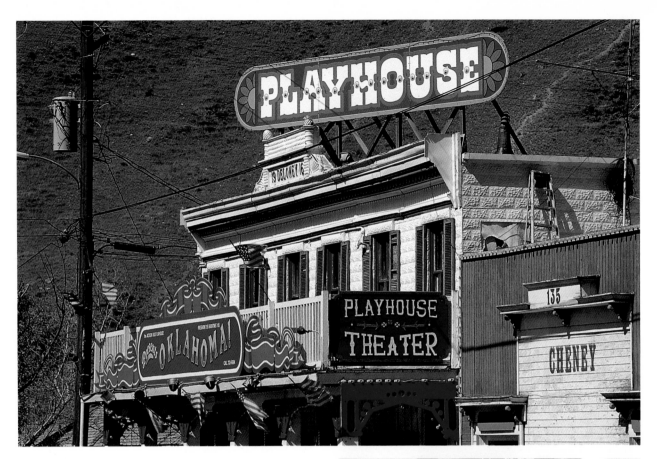

Among the many shops are stores that specialize in "Western" apparel ranging from cowboy boots to custom-made hats purchased by visitors and ranchers alike. For the person seeking cultural diversions, prowling the streets of Jackson is always a lively experience. Just north of town is the **National Wildlife Art Museum** housed in a spectacular rock edifice modeled after an ancient Indian cliff dwelling. The museum has become a major center for nature art exhibitions in the United States. Of course, if you want to get rowdy, there's always a night watching a musical stage production down at the **Playhouse Theater**.

The Playhouse is extremely popular with European visitors.

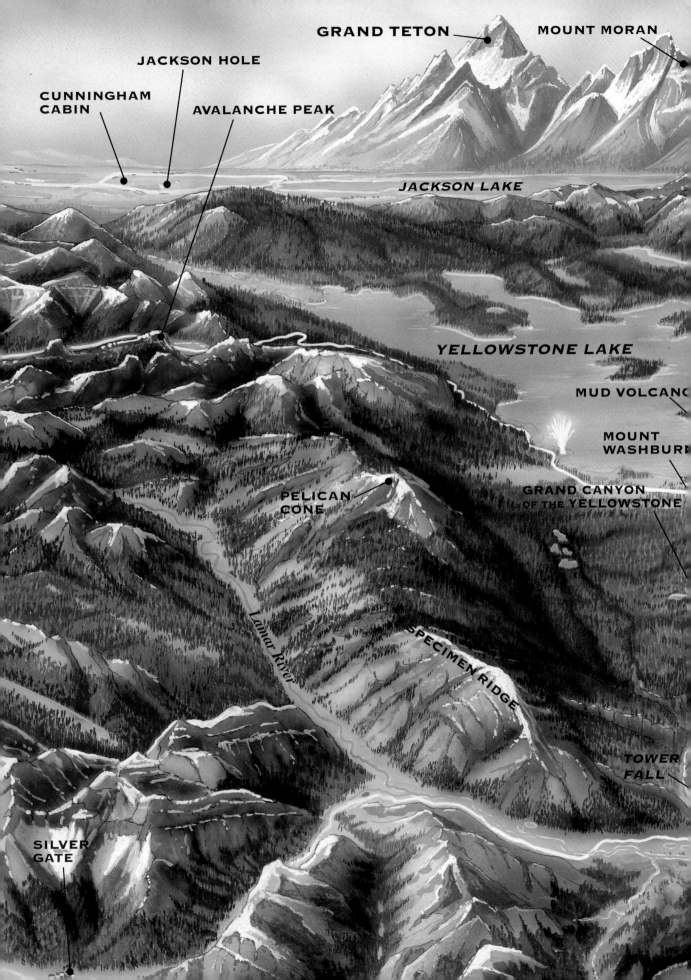

GRAND TETON

MOUNT MORAN

JACKSON HOLE

CUNNINGHAM CABIN

AVALANCHE PEAK

JACKSON LAKE

YELLOWSTONE LAKE

MUD VOLCANO

MOUNT WASHBURN

GRAND CANYON OF THE YELLOWSTONE

PELICAN CONE

Lamar River

SPECIMEN RIDGE

TOWER FALL

SILVER GATE

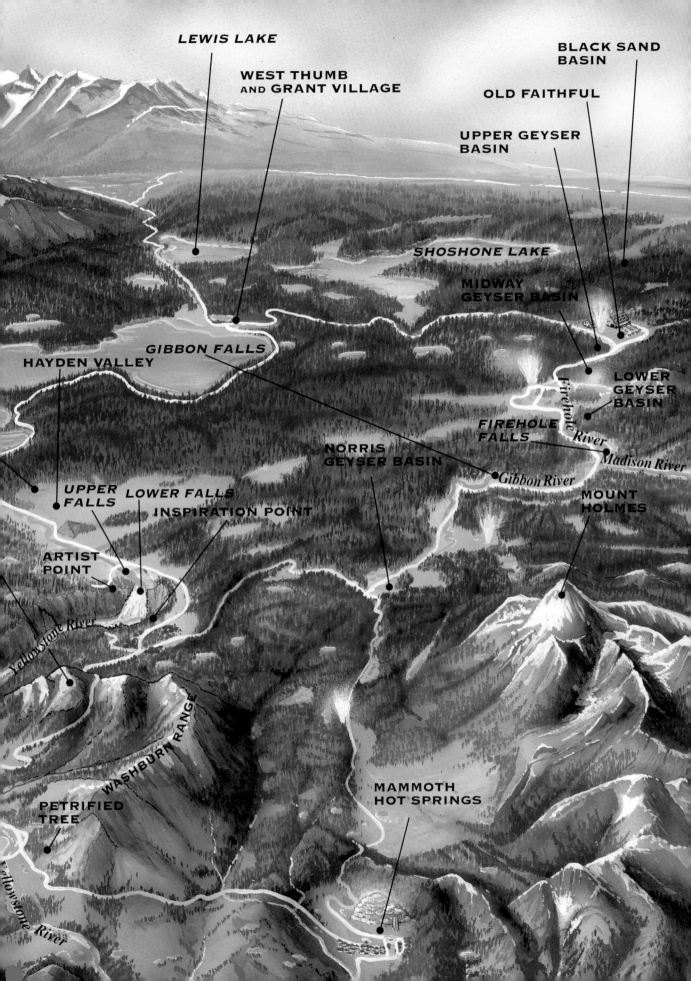

LEWIS LAKE

WEST THUMB AND GRANT VILLAGE

BLACK SAND BASIN

OLD FAITHFUL

UPPER GEYSER BASIN

SHOSHONE LAKE

MIDWAY GEYSER BASIN

GIBBON FALLS

HAYDEN VALLEY

LOWER GEYSER BASIN

Firehole River

FIREHOLE FALLS

Madison River

NORRIS GEYSER BASIN

Gibbon River

UPPER FALLS

LOWER FALLS

INSPIRATION POINT

MOUNT HOLMES

ARTIST POINT

Yellowstone River

WASHBURN RANGE

MAMMOTH HOT SPRINGS

PETRIFIED TREE

Yellowstone River

CONTENTS

YELLOWSTONE AND GRAND TETON NATIONAL PARKS

Project and editorial conception: Casa Editrice Bonechi
Picture research: Monica Bonechi
Graphic design: Manuela Ranfagni
Make-up: Laura Settesoldi
Editing: Anna Baldini *and* Simonetta Giorgi
Text: Todd Wilkinson
Maps: Studio Grafico Daniela Mariani, Pistoia
Drawing on pages 94/95: Stefano Benini

© Copyright by Casa Editrice Bonechi - Firenze - Italy

Printed in Italy by Centro Stampa Editoriale Bonechi.

The photographs belong to the Bonechi Archives and were taken by Andrea Pistolesi.
Historic photos on pages 3, 4, 5, 6: Record Group 79, National Archives and Records Administration, Yellowstone National Park.
Photos on page 11 bottom: Granata Press Service/IFA.
Photo on page 13 bottom left: Granata Press Service/Wildlife Collection/M. Francis.

ISBN 88-8029-321-4

Edition promoted by SMITH NOVELTY COMPANY, San Francisco

* * *